My First Transportation Books

TRUCKS GO!

Harold Morris

TABLE OF CONTENTS

A Crabtree Seedlings Book

CRABTREE
Publishing Company
www.crabtreebooks.com

Trucks

Pickup trucks are small. They carry light loads.

pickup truck
WASHINGTON
C14711K

Some trucks are tough.

They go in dirt and mud.

Firefighters drive **fire trucks**.

fire truck

They go fast to save the day.

Farmers use **dump trucks** to carry corn and wheat.

dump truck

delivery truck
The World on Time
fedex.com/hu
06 40 980 980

Delivery trucks bring packages to your door.

ice cream truck

Ice cream trucks bring ice cream.

Semi trucks are big.
They carry heavy loads.

semi truck
FREIGHTLINER
CZ·KP·57

Tow trucks help us when our cars won't go.

Then there are the really big trucks!

940

Glossary

delivery trucks (di-LIV-ur-ee TRUKS): Delivery trucks take things to homes and businesses.

dump trucks (DUHMP TRUKS): Dump trucks have a container on the back for carrying and unloading things.

fire trucks (FIRE TRUKS): Fire trucks have ladders and hoses to help firefighters put out fires.

pickup trucks (PIK-up TRUKS): Pickup trucks have an open space called a bed for carrying things.

semi trucks (SEM-i TRUKS): Semi trucks are big trucks made for carrying lots of items for long distances.

tow trucks (TOH TRUKS): Tow trucks lift up cars or trucks and pull them to other places.

Index

School-to-Home Support for Caregivers and Teachers

This book helps children grow by letting them practice reading. Here are a few guiding questions to help the reader build his or her comprehension skills. Possible answers appear here in red.

Before Reading

- **What do I think this book is about?** I think this book is about all kinds of trucks. I think this book is about how trucks can help people.
- **What do I want to learn about this topic?** I want to learn if special clothes or gear is needed to drive a truck. I want to learn if it's hard to drive a truck.

During Reading

- **I wonder why...** I wonder why some trucks can drive through dirt and mud. I wonder why semi trucks are so big.
- **What have I learned so far?** I have learned that there are delivery trucks that deliver packages. I have learned that tow trucks help us when our cars won't go.

After Reading

- **What details did I learn about this topic?** I have learned that pickup trucks are small and carry light loads. I have learned that farmers use large dump trucks to carry corn and wheat.
- **Read the book again and look for the glossary words.** I see the words *delivery trucks* on page 13, and the words *semi trucks* on page 16. The other glossary words are found on pages 22 and 23.

Library and Archives Canada Cataloguing in Publication

Available at the Library and Archives Canada

Library of Congress Cataloging-in-Publication Data

Available at the Library of Congress

Crabtree Publishing Company
www.crabtreebooks.com 1-800-387-7650
Print book version produced jointly with Blue Door Education in 2023

Written by: Harold Morris
Print coordinator: Katherine Berti
Printed in the U.S.A./072022/CG20220201

PHOTO CREDITS:
Cover and title page © IM_photo, Graham Cornall, page 4 inset photo © trangiap , pages 6-7 © sirtravelalot, pages 8-9 © blurAZ, pages 12-13 © Arsenie Krasnevsky, page 14 © anaglic, page 15 © Andrey_Kuzmin, pages 16-17 © Art Konovalov, page 18 © Baloncici, pages 20-21 © stocker_pro. All images from Shutterstock.com except page 2 © MCCAIG/istockphoto, large photo pages 4-5 © Ford Media www.fordtrucks.com, pages 10-11 © VR_Studio/istockphoto, page 19 © jondpatton/istockphoto

Published in the United States
Crabtree Publishing
347 Fifth Ave.
Suite 1402-145
New York, NY 10016

Published in Canada
Crabtree Publishing
616 Welland Ave.
St. Catharines, Ontario
L2M 5V6